Timeline of Ancient Egypt

Below you'll see some of the highs and lows of Egypt's long history, and meet some of the country's greatest heroes and villains.

Victory!
King Ahmose chases the Hyksos from Egypt and reclaims his country.

Laying to rest
Thutmosis I prepares the first royal tomb for himself in the Valley of the Kings.

Gloomy king
Gloomy King Senwosret III crushes the Nubians and settles old quarrels in Egypt.

1910BCE	1840BCE	1760BCE	1630BCE	1540BCE	1500BCE	1490BCE

Continued at back of book →

Karnak temple
Building starts on Karnak temple. It will become Egypt's greatest temple.

Disaster?
Hyksos kings rule the north of Egypt.

An obelisk at the central court of Karnak temple

Workmen's village
Deir el-Medina, the workmen's village, is created by Amenhotep I.

Ruins of the workmen's village

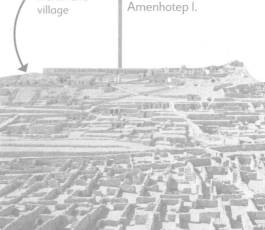

Woman ruler
Queen Nefrusobek is the first woman to rule officially as king, but her reign ends the Middle Kingdom.

Things to find out:

DK findout!

Ancient
Egypt

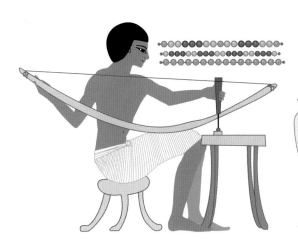

Author and consultant: Dr Angela McDonald

Penguin
Random
House

Editor Olivia Stanford
Project art editor Joanne Clark
Senior editor Jolyon Goddard
Design assistant Rhea Gaughan
Additional design Hoa Luc
Jacket co-ordinator Francesca Young
Jacket designer Amy Keast
Managing editor Laura Gilbert
Managing art editor Diane Peyton Jones
Pre-production producer Nadine King
Producer Srijana Gurung
Art director Martin Wilson
Publisher Sarah Larter
Publishing director Sophie Mitchell

Educational consultant Jacqueline Harris
Development consultant Dr Margaret Serpico

First published in Great Britain in 2017 by
Dorling Kindersley Limited
80 Strand, London, WC2R 0RL

Copyright © 2017 Dorling Kindersley Limited
A Penguin Random House Company
10 9 8 7 6 5 4 3 2 1
001–298645–Jan/2017

A CIP catalogue record for this book
is available from the British Library.
ISBN: 978-0-2412-8277-9

Printed and bound in China

A WORLD OF IDEAS:
SEE ALL THERE IS TO KNOW

www.dk.com

BCE/CE
When you see the letters BCE, it means years
Before the Common Era, which began in the
year 1CE (Common Era).

Contents

Cat mummy

Royal sandals

Faience beads

Scorpion

Dung beetle

Comb

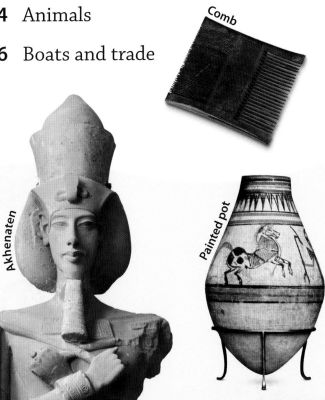
Akhenaten

Painted pot

Tutankhamun

The Ancient Egyptians

The Ancient Egyptians were people who lived in the lands around the River Nile thousands of years ago, in what is now modern-day Egypt. They loved their country, which they thought was the most advanced place in the world!

Why was the Nile so important?

The Nile's waters made life in the desert possible, creating a strip of green land where crops could grow along its banks. It also gave the Egyptians an easy way to travel the length of their country!

The main part of Ancient Egyptian history is divided into time spans called periods and kingdoms. During most of these spans, there were dynasties – family groups of kings who ruled the country.

» **Prehistoric Period:** 7000–5500BCE

» **Predynastic Period:** 5500–3100BCE

» **Early Dynastic Period:** 3100–2650BCE

» **Old Kingdom:** 2650–2175BCE

» **First Intermediate Period:** 2175–1975BCE

» **Middle Kingdom:** 1975–1755BCE

» **Second Intermediate Period:** 1755–1540BCE

» **New Kingdom:** 1540–1075BCE

» **Third Intermediate Period:** 1075–715BCE

» **Late Period:** 715–332BCE

» **Greco-Roman Period:** 332BCE–395CE

Where did they live?

The Egyptians lived where the land was sheltered on all sides – by the Mediterranean Sea to the north, deserts to the east and west, and rocky sections of the Nile, called cataracts, to the south.

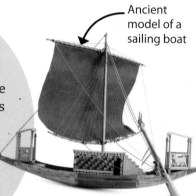

Ancient model of a sailing boat

The god Osiris was a symbol of the life-giving black mud of the Nile.

Emmer wheat

What did the Egyptians call Egypt?

The Ancient Egyptians called their country Kemet, meaning "Black land", after the black mud from the Nile that turned the desert into farmland. They called the surrounding desert Deshret, meaning "Red land".

The delta where the Nile runs into the sea is the greenest spot in Egypt.

Who was in charge?

In peaceful times, one Egyptian king or queen, called a pharaoh, ruled all of Egypt. However, there were unsettled times, and often the ruling pharaoh was from a foreign land that had conquered Egypt, especially towards the end of Ancient Egyptian history.

How long were they around?

The first traces of people living in Egypt are from 7000BCE, but the first pharaohs ruled from 3100BCE. Their civilization lasted for 3,000 years until Egypt became part of the Roman Empire.

Roman mummy portrait from 100CE

Under Roman rule, paintings of mummified people were done in a Roman style.

How big was the Egyptian Empire?

When it was at its biggest, the Egyptian Empire stretched from ancient Syria in the north down to Nubia in the south. This was under King Thutmosis III in the New Kingdom.

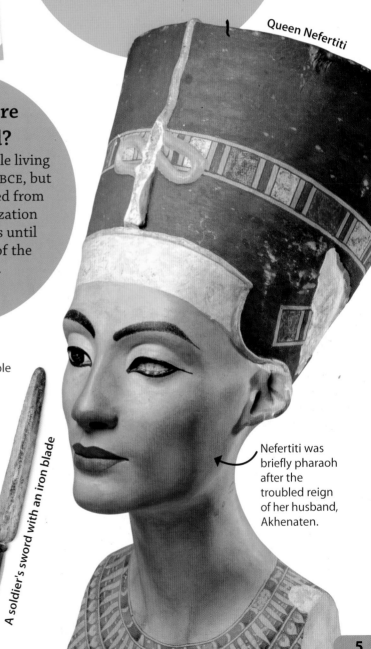

Queen Nefertiti

A soldier's sword with an iron blade

Nefertiti was briefly pharaoh after the troubled reign of her husband, Akhenaten.

Society

For most of ancient history, one pharaoh after another ruled Egypt. He or she was helped by family members and noblemen, all living in luxury. Everyone else worked very hard for this special group, doing as they were told and living simple lives, never even catching sight of their king.

Viziers

One or two prime ministers, called viziers, acted as "the eyes and ears of the king". They judged arguments, often about land, and managed Egypt's wealth.

Scribes

Only 1 in every 100 people could read and write, so scribes were very important. They wrote down everything to do with daily life.

Craftsmen

Craftsmen made everything from pots to beads. Although thousands of examples of works of art survive, they were not "signed", so we only know the names of a few craftsmen, such as the sculptor Irtysen.

Pharaoh

The pharaoh was a god to his people, and Egypt's success rested in his hands. A few women also ruled as pharaohs, such as Nefertiti and Hatshepsut, but this was unusual.

Priests and priestesses

Priests and priestesses ran temples dedicated to the gods. All priests shaved their heads and bodies. High priests could be as powerful as the pharaoh!

Slaves

Every Egyptian "belonged" to the pharaoh, but slaves were a special group. Most slaves were enemies captured in battles and made to work. Slavery was only common in the New Kingdom, which was a later part of Ancient Egyptian history.

A group of captives bound together

Soldiers

To reward their bravery, soldiers were given gifts of land and slaves, and could become very rich – if they survived in battle.

Merchants

Merchants worked for temples and brought exotic goods into the country, which they also traded with ordinary people.

! **WOW!**

Ancient Egyptian culture survived **nearly unchanged** for over **3,000 years!**

Farmers

Farmers were very important in Egyptian society as they produced food. They kept animals like cows and grew crops like wheat and barley. Most farmers didn't own their land, and they had to give away everything they grew.

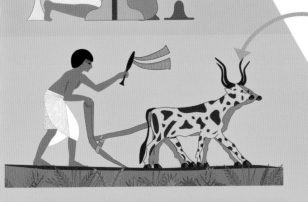

The Egyptian Empire

The Egyptian Empire was built around the River Nile. Under the warrior pharaohs of the New Kingdom, the Empire stretched deep down south into neighbouring Nubia and far up into the north-east. However, that meant clashes between the local people and the Egyptians, and Egypt made many enemies. Some of them even managed to take over Egypt – although never for long!

The pyramids
The most famous Egyptian landmarks, the pyramids were a tourist attraction even in ancient times!

The sphinx
King Khafre's guardian statue was a sphinx – a lion with the head of a man.

The Hittites

The Hittites rose to power during the New Kingdom. Pharaoh Ramses II couldn't defeat them, so he married a Hittite princess and craftily made them allies.

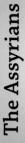

FROM THE NORTH-EAST

The Assyrians

The Assyrians were fierce warriors during the Late Period. They punished the Nubian-Egyptian king Taharka for interfering with their territories by destroying the great city of Thebes.

FROM THE EAST

The Hyksos

The Hyksos were nomads who settled in northern Egypt and ruled in the Second Intermediate Period. King Ahmose chased them out of Egypt and founded the New Kingdom.

Deir el-Medina
Deir el-Medina was a village for the workmen who made the tombs in the two royal valleys. They even built their own miniature pyramids, like this one.

Valley of the Queens
Smaller royal tombs for the pharaohs' wives, such as Nefertari, and children were found in the Valley of the Queens.

Red Sea

The Egyptian Empire, shown in yellow, on a map of the world

River Nile

Luxor temple
With its partner temple, Karnak, Luxor was a key spot for royal festivals.

Valley of the Kings
New Kingdom pharaohs were buried in the Valley of the Kings, including Tutankhamun.

The Egyptians
The Egyptians were always trying to expand their territory. Under strong kings, Nubia belonged to Egypt, but cities to the north were harder to hold on to.

FROM THE WEST

The Libyans
Several different groups of wandering nomads made up the Libyans. Some traded with the Egyptians, but many raided western Egyptian cities.

The Nubians
A proud people, the Nubians were often under Egyptian control. In the Late Period, a line of Nubian kings managed to conquer Egypt for a time.

FROM THE SOUTH

Soldiers and war

The early pharaohs used ordinary men to fight when they went to war against their enemies. But warrior kings such as Thutmosis III and Ramses II fought battle after battle, so they trained men to be soldiers. They even hired foreign soldiers, such as expert charioteers and fierce fighters, to help them build the Egyptian Empire.

Horses wore headdresses of ostrich feathers and ribbons.

Conquering kings

In this painting, the pharaoh Tutankhamun is shown in his war chariot, strong and fearless. When his tomb was discovered, it contained a golden chariot for him to ride in the afterlife.

Nubian army

Nubia was the land directly south of Ancient Egypt. The Egyptians called it the "Land of the Bow" because the Nubians were expert archers. They were often hired to fight alongside the Egyptians in battle.

Painted wooden statues of Nubian soldiers

Leopard-skin covering matches the king's clothes.

The king wears the Blue crown of war.

Guard protects the king's wrist from the bowstring.

Weapons

A soldier was only as strong as his weapons, which changed a lot during Egyptian history. Bronze weapons were replaced by stronger iron ones, designs were improved, and new technology – such as the chariot – was introduced.

Khepesh sword
This type of sword was introduced into Egypt from the north. Khepesh means "strength". The curved blade was light in weight, but sharp and deadly.

Flint arrowhead
Arrowheads were made of stone and sharpened to a very sharp point.

Dagger
This dagger has a golden handle and an iron blade. Soldiers strapped daggers to their waist.

Battleaxe
This long-bladed weapon was used for cutting or throwing. Axes with shorter blades eventually replaced this type of axe.

Pharaohs

Ancient Egypt's kings were called pharaohs, and every pharaoh had three tasks: to protect Egypt from the outside world, increase the size of the country by conquering neighbouring people, and keep the gods happy. All pharaohs wanted their names to live on in history, so they built huge temples and impressive tombs. Let's meet some of the most famous – and infamous – pharaohs!

KHUFU

Known for: The Great Pyramid of Giza

We only have one tiny statue left of Khufu to show us what he looked like. Egypt's biggest pyramid was built as a tomb and monument for this pharaoh. After his death, Khufu was remembered as a cruel man, who cared only about his pyramid and not his people.

The name of a pharaoh was written inside an oval shape, called a cartouche. Most pharaohs had more than one cartouche because they had more than one name.

AKHENATEN

Known for: Being totally unique

Akhenaten was a rebel pharaoh who outlawed all the gods except his sun god, the Aten. He founded a new capital city and introduced a strange new style of art. His odd-looking portraits fascinate us, but his people hated him and tried to smash all his images.

When did they rule?

The main part of Ancient Egyptian history is divided into three key time periods called "kingdoms". During each kingdom, a succession of pharaohs ruled over the whole country. There were unsettled periods between the kingdoms.

OLD KINGDOM

MIDDLE KINGDOM

Khufu
2551–2528 BCE

Between kingdoms there were unstable periods.

SENWOSRET III

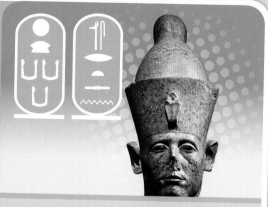

Known for: Being gloomy

Senwosret III was a harsh ruler who kept local governors firmly in their place. He built a chain of mighty fortresses in Nubia, south of Egypt, to control gold supplies and trade. Why do the statues of this pharaoh look so gloomy? Maybe it was because he worked so hard.

HATSHEPSUT

Known for: Being a woman-king!

This queen made herself into a king, showing herself as a man in works of art. Hatshepsut built new temples, but she was most proud of trading with the land of Punt, southeast of Egypt. She disappeared mysteriously when her nephew reached adulthood.

TUTANKHAMUN

Known for: Treasures!

Tutankhamun was the boy-king who returned Egypt to "normal" after the upheaval caused by his father, Akhenaten. Unfortunately, he died after only ten years of rule, at the age of 19. More than 3,000 treasures were crammed into his tiny tomb when it was opened in 1922CE.

RAMSES THE GREAT

Known for: Being big-headed

Ramses II, also known as "Ramses the Great", was a warrior king with more than 100 sons and daughters. This pharaoh carved his name all over Egypt – sometimes over the names of earlier pharaohs. In his temples, he worshipped the gods – and also himself!

Ramses the Great
1279–1213BCE

NEW KINGDOM

Senwosret III
336–1818BCE

Hatshepsut
1473–1458BCE

Akhenaten
1353–1336BCE

Tutankhamun
1332–1322BCE

Ruler of Egypt

Egypt's last pharaoh, Cleopatra VII, held her country together in difficult times. She stood up to the mighty Roman Empire, charming her way into the hearts of its greatest generals. Her beauty is legendary, even though her portraits paint her differently! Here's how an interview with her might have been.

Q: What was your childhood like?

A: It was unsettled! My family was always squabbling over who should be in power. Even as a girl, I knew it should be me.

Q: Did you expect to become pharaoh, then?

A: I wanted to be. After my father lost his throne, my mother and my sisters ruled before me briefly, but they weren't strong like me.

Coins were made with Cleopatra's face on them in her lifetime.

Q: What has been your proudest moment?

A: Outsmarting my brother – and enemy – Ptolemy to meet Julius Caesar, the leader of Rome. I smuggled myself into Ptolemy's palace, where Caesar was staying, wrapped in a carpet. You should have seen their faces when I appeared!

This head is thought to be of Cleopatra. It was carved in a classical Greek style.

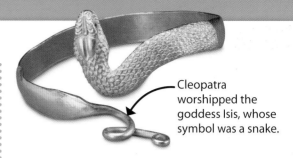

Cleopatra worshipped the goddess Isis, whose symbol was a snake.

Q: Do you think of yourself as Greek, like your ancestors, or Egyptian?

A: Both really. I'm Greek like Alexander the Great, my ancestor, but Egypt is in my heart. I'm the first in my family to learn the Egyptian language.

Q: Have you done a lot of travelling?

A: Oh yes! I've been up and down my own country, and far beyond. I went to Rome with Caesar and stayed in Arabia, Palestine, and Syria, when my horrid brother sent me away.

Q: Where is your favourite place?

A: It's the city of Alexandria, in Egypt. My palace there is wonderful, but there's also Ascalon, in Palestine. They loved me so much when I was there that they put my face on their coins.

Q: Do you see Rome as an ally or as a threat?

A: Well, Rome controls Egypt, so I've made sure it's my ally! I'm very good at charming its leaders – Caesar, Pompey, and Mark Antony.

Q: What will people remember about you in years to come?

A: My good looks and my determination! No matter what challenge life throws at me, I always find a way past it.

Q: What are your hopes for your children?

A: They're all going to be great leaders, just like me.

Q: Is there anything you're afraid of?

A: Losing my position. The people are so quick to riot, and I worry about Rome's new leader Octavian taking my beloved Egypt from me.

Cleopatra stands behind her and Julius Caesar's son, Caesarion, in a wall carving in the temple of Dendera.

Mysterious end

Soon after Octavian, later called Augustus, became Rome's leader, he put Cleopatra in prison. She died in 30BCE at the age of 39. Stories tell us a poisonous snake killed her, but the truth is still unknown. After Cleopatra's death, Egypt became part of the Roman Empire.

Pyramids

Pyramids were tombs for pharaohs when they died. These huge buildings protected the king's body and made sure he would never be forgotten. Building pyramids took years and required hundreds of men. Some kings died before their pyramid was finished. Other kings managed to build more than one pyramid.

How did they build them?

Here's how the building of the Great Pyramid at Giza might have looked. Stonemasons cut and shaped huge blocks of stone. Workers heaved them into place on wooden rollers along rubble ramps that clung to the sides of the pyramid.

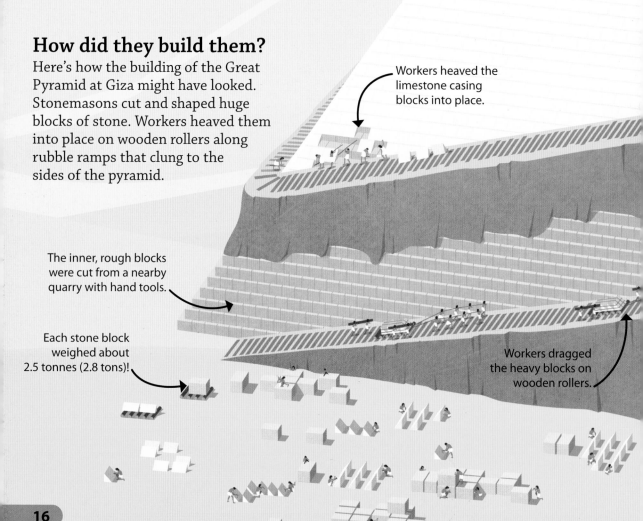

The capstone at the top was covered in electrum, a mixture of gold and silver.

Workers heaved the limestone casing blocks into place.

The inner, rough blocks were cut from a nearby quarry with hand tools.

Each stone block weighed about 2.5 tonnes (2.8 tons)!

Workers dragged the heavy blocks on wooden rollers.

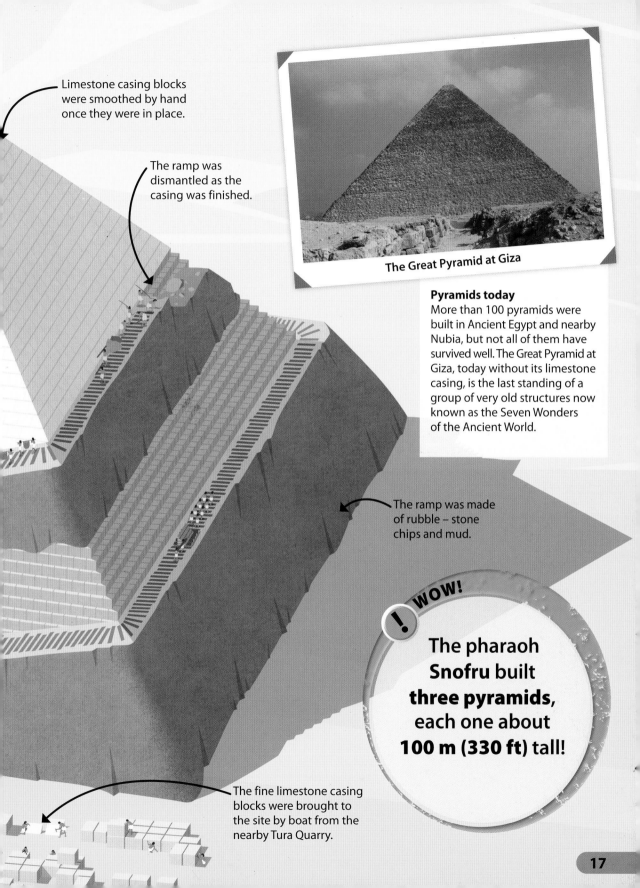

Limestone casing blocks were smoothed by hand once they were in place.

The ramp was dismantled as the casing was finished.

The Great Pyramid at Giza

Pyramids today
More than 100 pyramids were built in Ancient Egypt and nearby Nubia, but not all of them have survived well. The Great Pyramid at Giza, today without its limestone casing, is the last standing of a group of very old structures now known as the Seven Wonders of the Ancient World.

The ramp was made of rubble – stone chips and mud.

WOW!

The pharaoh **Snofru** built **three pyramids,** each one about **100 m (330 ft) tall!**

The fine limestone casing blocks were brought to the site by boat from the nearby Tura Quarry.

Making a mummy

The Egyptians believed that they still needed their physical body in order to have an afterlife. And not only that, it had to be perfect. It took nearly three months to make the body indestructible and beautiful. It could even have parts replaced – some mummies have been found with two left legs!

The priests who made mummies started by putting on jackal masks. They were making themselves into the jackal god Anubis, who they believed created the first ever mummy.

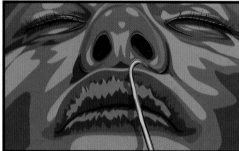

The brain was not thought to be important, so it was removed through the nose with a hook!

The lungs, stomach, liver, and intestines were carefully taken out of the body and put into special pots called canopic jars.

The body was then washed, inside and out, with sweet-smelling oils.

To dry out the body and stop it decaying, natron salt was poured all over the body and put inside it in bags. It took 40 days before the body was ready for the next stage.

Make-up and hair dye were used to make the body as beautiful as possible. Sometimes, the toenails and fingernails were covered with thin sheets of gold.

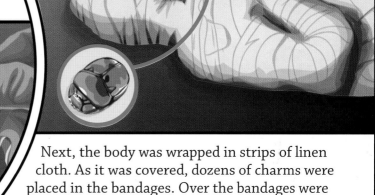

Next, the body was wrapped in strips of linen cloth. As it was covered, dozens of charms were placed in the bandages. Over the bandages were placed larger linen sheets.

Finally, a mask was put over the head and the body was placed in a coffin. Many coffins had human faces, always young and perfect, even if they belonged to a very old person!

Book of the Dead

Beautifully illustrated, this was a guidebook to the afterlife. It had many spells to keep a dead person safe or transform them into all sorts of things, and rules for when they met the gods.

Anubis prepares the mummy
A priest dressed as the god Anubis makes the dead person into a mummy. Their journey begins.

Negative confession
In the underworld, the dead person meets the gods. In the negative confession, they must tell the gods they've done nothing bad during their life.

Weighing of the heart
To get to paradise, the dead person must pass a test. Their heart must weigh exactly the same as the Feather of Justice. However, if it doesn't…

Journey of the dead

When a person died, their journey into the afterlife began. The Egyptians imagined the afterlife as a maze of roads, with gates to pass through and gods to please along the way. Every dead person had to pass a test before they were allowed into the afterlife. If they passed the test, they became very powerful.

Facing the monster
… the heavy, wicked heart is tossed to the monster Ammut, who gobbles it up. For these people, their journey now ends.

Paradise at last
The journey ends in the kingdom of the dead, where there are flowers, food, and everything anyone could ever want.

5

Passed the test!
Good people escape the monster and become very powerful. They are able to turn themselves into anything, including a snake with legs!

Body and spirit

A person's spirit, known as the Ba, looked like a bird with a human head. It could fly out into the world of the living. A dead person needed special spells to make it come back to them in the afterlife!

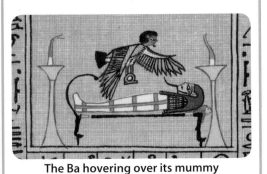

The Ba hovering over its mummy

Royal burial

Kings did not have to pass a test, like ordinary people. They joined the sun god and sailed across the sky forever. Treasure was buried with them – even their coffins were covered in gold. All the coffins below belonged to the pharaoh Tutankhamun.

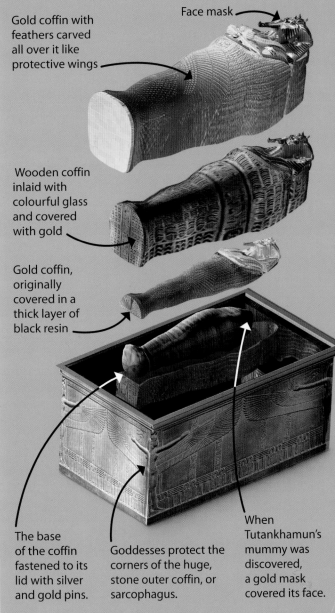

Gold coffin with feathers carved all over it like protective wings

Face mask

Wooden coffin inlaid with colourful glass and covered with gold

Gold coffin, originally covered in a thick layer of black resin

The base of the coffin fastened to its lid with silver and gold pins.

Goddesses protect the corners of the huge, stone outer coffin, or sarcophagus.

When Tutankhamun's mummy was discovered, a gold mask covered its face.

Tour of the tombs

Valley of the Kings

During the time known as the New Kingdom, kings stopped building pyramids. Instead, the royal family was buried in huge rock-cut tombs in two guarded valleys, called the Valley of the Kings and the Valley of the Queens. The tombs had colourful paintings, treasures for the afterlife, and booby traps just in case robbers broke into them!

Valley of the Kings

This map shows the tombs in the main part of the Valley of the Kings, known as the East Valley. There is also a smaller West Valley with a few tombs. So far, we know of 65 tombs in total, but new ones are still being discovered!

Valley of the Queens

This valley, for royal wives and children, is smaller than the Valley of the Kings, but it contains more tombs – about 90. Its star attraction is the tomb of Nefertari, the wife of Ramses II. Its paintings were restored in 1992 and now look brand new.

Nefertari

Thutmosis III

This warrior king was creative when it came to his tomb, numbered KV34. Its entrance is unusually high up in a cliff face, and the burial chamber is shaped like an oval cartouche.

The king's stone coffin, or sarcophagus

KV 34

Tutankhamun

The most famous tomb in the valley, KV62, was discovered in 1922. It was still full of treasures and held Tutankhamun's body. It had been robbed twice in the distant past, but sealed up again.

One of Tutankhamun's golden thrones

KV 62

KV 55

KV 17

KV stands for "Kings' Valley".

Mystery tomb

In the tomb numbered KV55, a coffin was found with its face and all names on it hacked away. Some Egyptologists think that this might be the tomb of the hated king Akhenaten.

This coffin in KV55 was deliberately damaged.

Seti I

The most beautiful tomb in the Valley of the Kings, KV17, belonged to Seti I. It is the longest and deepest tomb, famous for its painting of the night sky and stars on its ceiling.

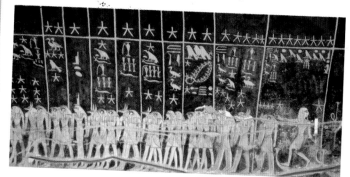

The gods of the night sky

At home

Towns in Ancient Egypt were built on the edges of the River Nile, and modern towns have been built right on top of them, so there's not much left of the ancient towns to tell us what the houses were like. But the village of Deir el-Medina, built in the desert beside the valleys containing the royal tombs, shows us what everyday life was like.

House in Deir el-Medina

The builders who built the royal tombs lived in Deir el-Medina with their families. This picture shows a typical medium-sized house in the village. About 20 people would have lived in it!

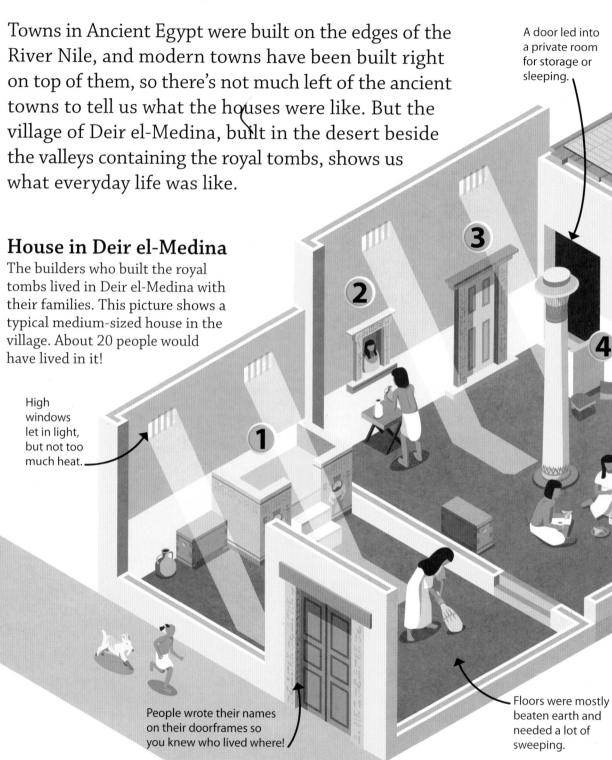

A door led into a private room for storage or sleeping.

High windows let in light, but not too much heat.

People wrote their names on their doorframes so you knew who lived where!

Floors were mostly beaten earth and needed a lot of sweeping.

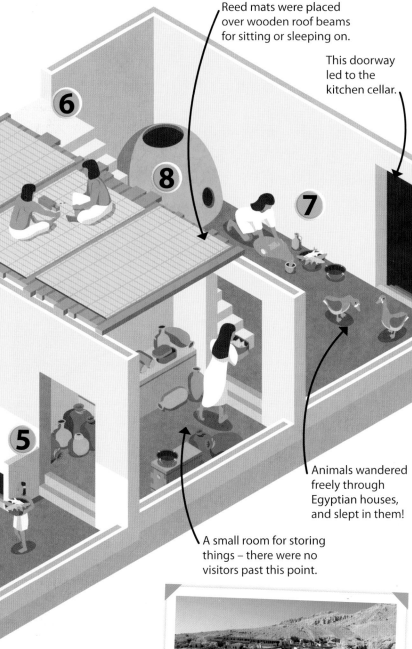

Reed mats were placed over wooden roof beams for sitting or sleeping on.

This doorway led to the kitchen cellar.

Animals wandered freely through Egyptian houses, and slept in them!

A small room for storing things – there were no visitors past this point.

Workmen's village
Deir el-Medina is almost perfectly preserved because it's in such a difficult spot to get to and no later buildings were built over it. Supplies and especially water had to be brought to the villagers.

Village of Deir el-Medina today

WHAT'S INSIDE

1 **Enclosed bed** This mysterious structure might have been used for sleeping or praying, but we don't know!

2 **Household shrine** This could contain a family statue. The household prayed here and made offerings to the gods.

3 **False door** A fake door set into the wall was another place for praying. It also let the ghosts of past family members, whom the Egyptians believed visited them, into the house.

4 **Seating area** Guests were seated in the fanciest of the rooms.

5 **Cellar** Steps led down to a cellar, where treasured possessions could be kept safe.

6 **Steps to roof** Egyptian houses had flat roofs with steps up to them. People might sleep here at night.

7 **Quernstone** Grain was ground into flour using a roller and a flat stone called a quernstone.

8 **Oven** An open-topped oven was used for baking bread – all Egyptian homes made their own bread.

Artwork

Egyptian art is usually very colourful and beautiful, but every piece of art also had a very important job to do – to preserve, to protect, or to provide. Many pieces "speak", which means they have words on them. Every item was made to last forever and many pieces look as bright today as the day they were made.

Wall paintings

Paintings on tomb walls often preserved the tomb owner's image and wishes for the afterlife. These might include being close to the gods, such as Osiris, above. Gods and people were shown with their body facing out and their head looking to the side.

What is papyrus?

Papyrus is a marsh plant that grows on the banks of the Nile. The Egyptians tore its stalks into strips, flattened them, and stuck them together to form sheets of paper also known as papyrus.

Papyrus

This sheet of papyrus is from the Book of the Dead, which provided spells and knowledge for a person's journey to the afterlife. Here, the sun-god Khepri is shown as a winged scarab beetle travelling across the sky.

Statues

Pharaohs often had themselves carved as statues. The biggest statue ever made in Egypt was the huge lion-bodied sphinx with King Khafre's head. Its job was to protect his tomb.

Pottery

Pottery could be useful or decorative. Beautiful pieces were often made for use in the afterlife. The writing on this blue perfume jar is the name of the king Amenhotep II. It could have belonged to him or been a gift from him.

Wood carvings

The Egyptians carved little servant figures, called shabtis, to be put into their tombs to serve them in the afterlife. The spell written on this figure brings her to life, and she will shout "I'll do it!" for every task given to her.

27

Gods

The Egyptians believed in over 100 gods and goddesses – they even borrowed some from their neighbours! Many stayed popular for thousands of years. Some gods were shown with the heads or bodies of animals, and most wore a special symbol on their heads to show who they were.

Family tree

Many of the gods and goddesses belonged to family groups. This is one of the best known. Each god in it represented part of the natural world, such as the sky and stars.

God of the Sun

Atum Ra was the father of the gods. He created himself and then the world from a watery nothingness.

ATUM RA

Goddess of water

Lion-headed and a little bit fierce, Tefnut represented the water that the Egyptians needed to survive.

TEFNUT

Goddess of the sky and stars

Nut's body was home to the stars and the Sun. She was usually shown stretched over Geb, just touching him with her fingers and toes.

NUT

God of the air

Shu represented the atmosphere. His name means "air" and "light". The Egyptians called clouds the "bones of Shu".

SHU

God of the Earth

Geb was the son of air and water. He was often drawn lying flat on his back in order to support his wife, Nut, who was the sky.

GEB

SETH

God of violence

Strong, but jealous of his brother Osiris, Seth tried to steal the throne from him. Later he made peace with Osiris's son and heir, Horus.

NEPHTHYS

Goddess of protection

Nephthys was a kind goddess. She comforted her sister Isis after her husband Osiris died, and she helped her bring him back to life.

Hathor

Another important goddess was Hathor. She was very beautiful and loved music, dancing, and beer! Homesick Egyptians who had travelled to faraway places built temples for her so she would protect them. She is often shown as a cow carrying the Sun between its horns.

Hathor with cow's horns holding the Sun

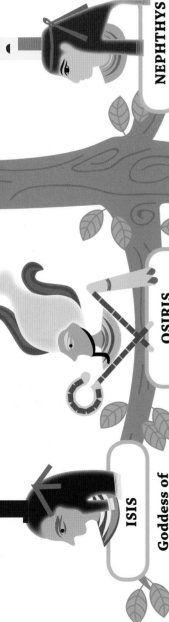

ISIS

Goddess of magic and life

Isis was a loving wife and mother, but also a powerful magician. She was one of Egypt's most popular and longest-lived goddesses. Even the Romans loved her!

OSIRIS

God of the dead

Osiris was Egypt's first king. When he died he became master of the afterlife, which meant he got to decide who lived in his underworld kingdom after death.

ANUBIS

God of embalming

The son of Nephthys, this jackal-headed god looked after the bodies of the dead. He created the first mummy from the body of Osiris.

HORUS

God of the sky and kingship

As a boy, Horus fought his uncle Seth and won the throne of Egypt. He became protector of the pharaohs.

Temples

The temples of Egypt ranged from small, rock-cut shrines, to massive complexes the size of small towns. As the homes of the gods, they were very secret places. They were filled with statues, music, and the smell of incense, but not worshippers. Only the pharaoh and the gods' servants – priests and priestesses – were allowed inside.

Luxor

A festival called Opet was held each year at the temple of Luxor. During the festival, a huge procession brought a statue of the god Amun from his temple in nearby Karnak to visit Luxor. Two rows of sphinxes lined the route. Ramses II put huge statues of himself at the entrance so he'd always be the first to welcome the god.

Row of sphinxes

Other temples

As well as Luxor, there were more than 100 other temples built in Ancient Egypt. Some of these temples can still be visited today.

Karnak

Karnak
Three temples in one, Karnak is the largest temple complex in Egypt. It was dedicated to the god Amun and his family.

Edfu
Egypt's best preserved temple is Edfu. Falcons sacred to the god Horus were looked after there.

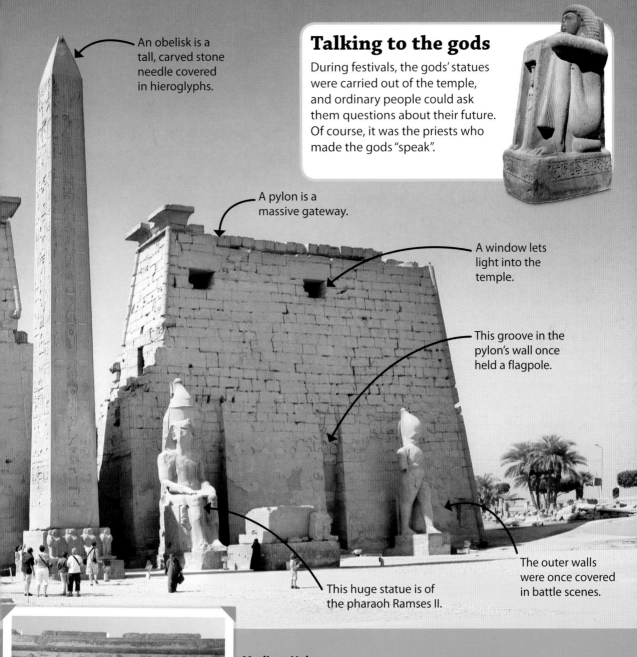

An obelisk is a tall, carved stone needle covered in hieroglyphs.

Talking to the gods

During festivals, the gods' statues were carried out of the temple, and ordinary people could ask them questions about their future. Of course, it was the priests who made the gods "speak".

A pylon is a massive gateway.

A window lets light into the temple.

This groove in the pylon's wall once held a flagpole.

This huge statue is of the pharaoh Ramses II.

The outer walls were once covered in battle scenes.

Medinet Habu

Medinet Habu
Wonderful colours survive inside Medinet Habu. It is dedicated to the memory of the powerful pharaoh Ramses III.

Dendera
The temple of Dendera contains an amazing ceiling painted like the night sky. It also has pillars topped with the face of the goddess Hathor.

Egyptian clothes

Egyptian women made their own linen cloth from a plant called flax. Flax fibres were soaked, scrubbed, and then spun into thread that was woven into fabric. Priests wore animal furs. Woollen clothing was rare as it would have made the person wearing it too hot!

Headband made of beads

The beaded necklace was a symbol of beauty.

Tight-fitting dress underneath the see-through robe

Women
Wealthy women wore long dresses of very fine white linen. At first, tight dresses were in fashion, but later, flowing dresses with pleated folds became popular.

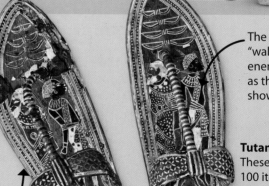

Royal shoes and crowns
A king had to look different from everyone else to show his high status. He sometimes wore richly decorated sandals and had more than one type of crown.

The sandals were decorated with pictures of Egypt's enemies.

The king would "walk" on his enemies, such as the Nubian shown here.

Tutankhamun's shoes
These are among nearly 100 items of footwear found in Tutankhamun's tomb. They are made of wood and leather, with gold decoration.

Layered wig

Multi-coloured wig, edged with gold

Fine wraparound kilt with sash belt

The kilt (skirt) was worn underneath a fine linen robe.

Feet usually bare

Men

All men wore short linen kilts. In later times, the wealthy wore very finely spun linen wrappings over the kilts. Rich men also sometimes wore sandals.

Gods

The gods' clothes were very similar to ordinary people's, with kilts for gods and dresses for goddesses. However, they were much more colourful and fancy.

Red crown
The Red crown represented the north of Egypt, also called Lower Egypt. It was probably made of leather and dyed with red ochre, a type of mineral.

Blue crown
The Blue crown was worn by kings in battle or out hunting. It had a rearing cobra, known as the uraeus, at the front and little circles studded in its dyed leather.

White crown
The partner of the Red crown, the White crown represented the south, or Upper Egypt. It may have been made from stiff white linen, but no crowns actually survive.

33

Beauty

All sorts of items have survived to tell us the beauty secrets of the Ancient Egyptians. Eyes and lips were brightened with colour, fancy wigs were soaked with perfume, and decorative beads were worn. Looking good was definitely an art – for both men and women!

Perfume cone

Perfume
The secret to perfect hair was a strange cone on your head! These cones were made of wax mixed with perfume. During the evening they melted into your hair, making it look shiny and smell nice.

Hair
Most of the beautiful hairstyles we see in paintings and on statues are actually wigs! Wigs were easier to style and might have been thought to be cleaner. Egyptians used razors to shave off their real hair.

Narrow teeth

Comb
This double-sided comb had wide teeth for brushing, and narrow teeth for combing out lice!

Green malachite powder

Black kohl was used as eye make-up and as medicine!

Eyes

Eyes were decorated for beauty, but also because it was thought to keep them healthy. Green powder was made from the mineral malachite and kohl was made from galena, another mineral. Both men and women painted their eyes.

The sharp end was used for mixing; the flat end was used for putting on colour.

Alabaster kohl pot with lid

Kohl tubes

Kohl was often stored in tubes, just like eyeliner today. These could be made of wood, stone, or faience, a glass-like material. A stick was used to apply the kohl.

Tweezers were used to remove stray hairs.

Kohl stick shaped like an arm

Lips

Red paint was used on the lips but not on the cheeks, as pale faces were the height of fashion for ladies, and red lips made a nice contrast. Paint was made from grinding up a red mineral called haematite.

Razor

A razor was used for removing hair from anywhere on the body to keep it cool and clean.

Powdered red haematite

Mirrors were made of copper or bronze. The polished metal has become dark over time.

Jewellery

In Ancient Egypt, jewellery wasn't just decorative. It could tell others of your high position within society, especially if it was a gift from the king and had his name on it. The Egyptians also believed that some objects were magical and could protect you from harm.

Carved centre called a bezel

Bracelet
This bracelet is made from blue faience beads and shells, with a little cat amulet representing the goddess Bastet.

Finger rings
Rings could be used as seals – they were pressed into soft clay to leave a stamp. They often had unique designs.

This pendant carved in the shape of the eye of Horus is upside down.

Scarab mystery

What is the yellowish scarab beetle in this pectoral found in Tutankhamun's tomb made of? Scientists have suggested that the stone in this large chest pendant might have come from a lightning strike in the desert, turning sand into glass, or even from a meteorite!

Tutankhamun's pectoral

Earrings
These attached to either side of the ear rather than going through it like a modern earring. They could also be worn in the hair.

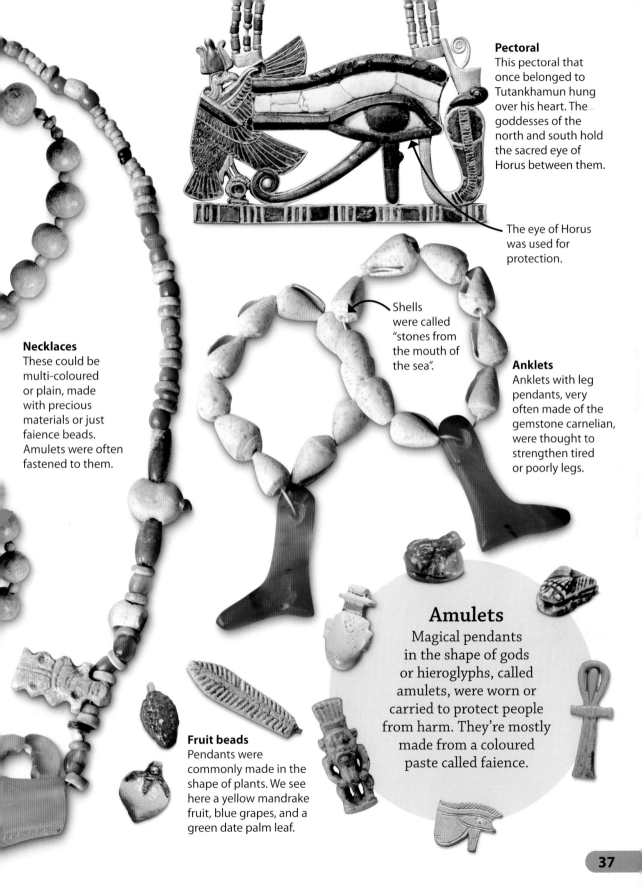

Pectoral
This pectoral that once belonged to Tutankhamun hung over his heart. The goddesses of the north and south hold the sacred eye of Horus between them.

The eye of Horus was used for protection.

Shells were called "stones from the mouth of the sea".

Necklaces
These could be multi-coloured or plain, made with precious materials or just faience beads. Amulets were often fastened to them.

Anklets
Anklets with leg pendants, very often made of the gemstone carnelian, were thought to strengthen tired or poorly legs.

Amulets
Magical pendants in the shape of gods or hieroglyphs, called amulets, were worn or carried to protect people from harm. They're mostly made from a coloured paste called faience.

Fruit beads
Pendants were commonly made in the shape of plants. We see here a yellow mandrake fruit, blue grapes, and a green date palm leaf.

Egyptian jobs

In Ancient Egypt, your family played a big part in the job you did. If your father was rich, you would follow in his footsteps and become an important official. If your father was a farmer? Well, you'd probably be one too. But if you were really ambitious, even if your family was poor, you could make your own dreams come true and rise up the ranks.

Metalworker

Metalworkers had to put up with hot, fiery furnaces as they melted down copper, gold, silver, and eventually iron to make everything from sturdy weapons to dainty pendants.

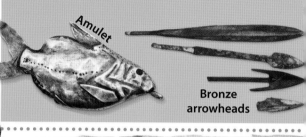

Amulet

Bronze
arrowheads

Scribe

Writing palette

Very few people could read and write, so scribes knew they were important and often boasted about their "clever fingers". They did all sorts of jobs, from recording the pharaoh's glorious deeds in battle to writing receipts for donkey sales.

BOATMAN

A single boatman could sail a simple riverboat a short distance. Bigger ships going further needed a bigger crew, including oarsmen, a captain, and a sailor to guide the rudder at the rear. Sometimes, a musician helped the oarsmen row in time!

Model boat with crew, made for the afterlife

Potter

People who make objects out of clay are called potters. In Egypt, they needed a good eye for the best quality of clay and the skills to shape it with simple tools. They made dishes, statues, and even coffins.

Scorpion charmer

Workers known as "controllers of the scorpion goddess Selket" used magical powers to chase off the dangerous animals in the desert. These workers were usually part of mining expeditions and also treated stings and bites.

A sting from a scorpion is extremely painful. ➤

Temple of Ramses II, Abu Simbel, Egypt

Comedian

You might even become a comedian in Ancient Egypt. A funny man named Ahanakht left an inscription in a quarry describing himself: "I'm a dancer, I'm a beloved prancer. I'm the joy of his company, a man loved by his whole town. There's never a sad face in it!"

Priestess

Alongside their duties at home, high-ranking women could become priestesses in temples. They were very often dancers and singers who entertained the gods. In the city of Thebes, royal women took the role of "Wife of the God Amun" and practically ran the city.

Architect

The most important architect was called the "Overseer of All Works". He designed palaces, tombs, temples, and sometimes even towns. The best architects knew how to create clever twists in tombs to trap would-be tomb robbers. They also knew how to guide sunlight along a shaft into a dark room as a dramatic flourish. Two royal architects even became gods in later times.

Farming

Egyptian farmers depended on the River Nile. Each year, flood waters from the south, known as the Inundation, left behind rich black mud, which turned the Egyptian desert into farmland. The Nile's height was carefully measured – too high or too low would mean disaster for farmers and their crops.

Egyptian seasons

There were three seasons in the Egyptian year: Akhet, Peret, and Shemu. An Egyptian year had 365 days, but no leap years. This meant it gradually fell out of step with the seasons. When they matched again, there was great celebration!

Shemu – Harvest
Mid-February to mid-June

Shemu
The hot summer sun ripened crops and then it was time to gather them in. During the harvest, seeds were collected for the next year's planting.

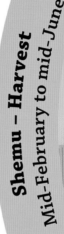

REALLY?

The River Nile was never worshipped – but **the Inundation** was celebrated as **a god!**

Akhet – Flooding
Mid-June to mid-October

Akhet
The year began in mid-June, when the Nile's waters rose. This was the time to build – you couldn't farm when the land was underwater!

Peret
Crops, such as wheat, were planted as soon as the land emerged from the flood. This was the busiest season for farmers.

Fertile Nile

The famous Ancient Greek traveller Herodotus called Egypt the "gift of the Nile" because without its floodwaters the land would just be a desert.

Farmers today grow sugar cane along the Nile.

Peret – Growth
Mid-October to mid-February

Food and drink

In Egypt's fertile soil, lots of fruit, vegetables, and cereal crops, such as wheat, thrived. The rich could spoil themselves with extra-tasty treats, but even poor Egyptians ate well. We still eat many of the same foods the Ancient Egyptians enjoyed.

Food for the poor

The poor mainly existed on a simple diet of bread and beer, which they made themselves. Some also grew their own fruit and vegetables.

Lettuce
Lettuce was used as a food, a medicine, and even as an offering for the gods!

Beer
Even children drank beer in Ancient Egypt. However, it was thick and soupy, to fill you up rather than to make you drunk!

Spring onions
From early times, spring onions were a major part of the diet of poor Egyptians.

Nabk fruit
These small fruit grew on thorn trees and tasted like apples.

Radish
Easily grown, but tough to eat, Egyptian radishes were probably boiled before eating.

Cucumber
The fanciest food on the menu – cucumber would have been an occasional treat!

Bread
The most common food, bread came in all sorts of shapes and sizes.

Food for the rich

Sweet cakes, sticky pastries, rich meat dishes, and all the fresh fruit and vegetables they liked: rich Egyptians ate a much more varied diet than the poor. The main difference in their diets was that the wealthy ate much more meat.

REALLY?

A rich Egyptian called Mereruka had **hyenas** fattened for a feast!

Meat
Beef was the most prized meat and only for the rich, but all sorts of animals were eaten, such as pigeon.

Cake
Cakes came in all shapes and were flavoured with fruits, seeds, and nuts.

Pomegranate
Pomegranates had to be traded as they didn't grow in Egypt.

Melons
Both the fruit and the seeds of melons were eaten.

Lotus root
Crunchy and a bit sharp-tasting, lotus roots were eaten raw or cooked.

Yoghurt
Because milk didn't keep well in the hot Egyptian sun, it was made into yoghurt and cheese.

Honey
Honey was used like sugar to sweeten food and drinks.

Dates
Dates were eaten on their own or mashed into jam for cakes.

Figs
Sycamore figs were especially prized and made into a strong wine.

Animals

The Egyptians were surrounded by animals. They kept them as pets, raised them for food, and used them to carry loads or plough fields. Dangerous animals, such as lions, were hunted – or avoided! Others, such as ibises, became symbols of the gods. These animals lived in temples and were mummified when they died.

Lion
Pharaohs admired the lion's strength so much that they created sphinxes – statues with their own heads on lion bodies.

Ibis
This waterbird represented the writer god Thoth, maybe because its long beak made marks in the mud like a pen.

Baboon
Although bad-tempered, baboons were popular pets in Ancient Egypt.

Hippopotamus
This fierce river animal was a threat to fishermen. It was one of many animals of the god Seth.

Cat
Much loved, cats were worshipped in later times as the symbol of the goddess Bastet.

Dung or scarab beetle
Pushing a ball of dung around, this insect represented the sun god travelling across the sky.

Crocodile
The crocodile was the terror of boatmen on the Nile and grazing animals on the shore. It was worshipped as the god Sobek.

Falcon
Known as the "lord of the sky", the falcon was the symbol of the god Horus and the pharaoh.

Jackal
The jackal was seen at night in cemeteries. It became the symbol of the god Anubis, who looked after the dead.

Match the mummy

In the final stages of Ancient Egyptian history, millions of animals were made into mummies as offerings to the gods they stood for. Can you unravel the mystery and match each mummy with the animal inside it?

1

2

3

4

Fish **A**

Ibis **B**

Cat **C**

Crocodile **D**

Boats and trade

Most Egyptian boats were for short journeys on the Nile. But bigger ships were built for sea voyages that took soldiers and merchants to faraway places. Sometimes there was fighting, but often the aim was trade for necessities like cedar wood for buildings or luxuries like precious metals, stones, and spices.

Hatshepsut's boat

Queen Hatshepsut's ships brought all sorts of exotic objects and animals from the faraway land of Punt. Most precious were the incense trees for her temple garden.

WOW!

Five **life-sized** ships were buried with King Khufu – one was **43.3 m (142 ft) long!**

Strong ropes held the mast in place.

Lookout positions were at both ends of the ship.

An anchor was dropped from the prow to stop the ship floating away.

Ropes wrapped round the ship held the hull to the ship's inner frame.

The sail, here rolled up, was made of the cloth linen.

The stern of the ship was shaped like a lotus plant.

The rudder was used to steer the ship.

WHAT'S ON BOARD?

1 Incense trees These were precious because they didn't grow in Egypt. Incense was burned to please the gods, so it was very important.

2 Unusual pets Baboons and green monkeys were brought to Egypt to be kept as pets.

3 Ebony This glossy, dark wood was perfect for making special items of furniture.

4 Ivory Tusks from African elephants were made into ivory figurines and containers.

5 Leopard skins These were used for clothing and decorating things like quivers, which held arrows.

6 Storage jars and sacks Scented myrrh resin, gold, minerals to be ground down for paint, and exotic herbs were moved in jars and sacks.

7 People from Punt Adults and children were part of the ship's cargo. They might have travelled to Egypt to help look after the incense trees.

Medicine

Quite a few Ancient Egyptian books, called papyri, have survived that are filled with all kinds of remedies for curing illnesses and treating injuries. Egyptian doctors were clever, and some of their remedies, such as honey, are still used today. Many medicines, however, were very strange. Don't try any of these at home!

Do you have a wound?

Bandage it with meat!

Wounds from cuts and bites were bandaged up as soon as possible with fresh meat.

Do you have trouble seeing?

Use a pig's eye!

Actually, just the liquid from inside the pig's eye was needed – and it was poured into the person's ear!

Did a snake bite you?

Get some beer!

The beer wasn't for drinking. An onion was crushed up in it and the mixture was gargled for a whole day!

Do you have a headache?

Boil a catfish!

The catfish's skull was boiled in oil, and the mixture was rubbed on the aching head for four days.

Are your eyes sore?

Put on some make-up!

Powdered eye paints were used as medicine to keep eyes healthy and free from flies.

Have you got a splinter?

Use sea salt and wasp dung!

These were mixed with dough, fat, red lead powder, and wax, and then smeared on the splinter.

Are your eyelashes curling in?

Use lizard's blood!

Lashes that curled in were pulled out, and the area was treated with lizard's and bat's blood, and incense.

Magic

Many medicines had ingredients that were chosen because they were believed to be magical. Spells were often said as medicines were taken, too.

Magic wand
Fierce creatures were carved into ivory "wands" to chase harm away, especially from the ill or the very young.

Horus stele
Water was poured over this decorated stone, called a stele, to soak up its magical spells. The water was then drunk to protect against dangerous animals.

Magic spell
This real Egyptian magical spell was used after a nightmare. The bad god Seth and the good god Re are mentioned in it.

"Welcome, good dream! May night be seen as day! May all sufferings caused by Seth, the son of Nut, be driven out! Re is victorious over his enemies, and I am victorious over my enemies!"

Roll a dice to play the game of childhood!

START

You've been born!

Life is hard for the very young in Ancient Egypt. You'll be given a name to bring you luck throughout your life, such as "He will be happy".

1 **Your mother is a slave. Miss a go!**
If your parents are slaves, you'll be one too. You'll have to work hard for the people who own you.

2

13

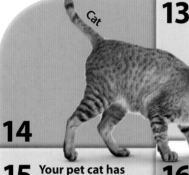

Cat

12 **You're a natural redhead. Have another go!**
Red hair is rare in Egypt and a symbol of the god Seth.

11

Ankh amulet

14

15 **Your pet cat has scratched you. Miss a go!**
Your family might have a lot of pets, such as cats, dogs, or even something like a gazelle, baboon, or green monkey.

16 **Bes answers your prayers. Move forwards 3 places.**
The fierce god Bes looks after all children. Make sure his image is always close to you and you'll be fine.

17

Bes jug

18 **You're feeling unwell. Miss a g**
Sometimes the medicin you get from the docto makes you feel worse than the actual illness! Let's hope it doesn't contain dung…

Children in Egypt

In Ancient Egypt, children had to grow up fast, whether they were rich or poor. There were many dangers around them, including illnesses and wild animals. The Egyptians loved and cared for their children and believed the gods protected them, too. Play this game to find out about childhood in Egypt.

27 **Lucky scarab. Have another g**

28

Senet game

3 **You've been given a hedgehog rattle. Move forwards 1 place.** Real toys in Ancient Egypt are rare. Children don't get a lot of time to play…

4 Hedgehog rattle

5 **Your family are farmers and you have to work in the fields. Go back 3 places.** As a farmer's child, you'll learn by working alongside your family from an early age.

6

The children of farmers helped harvest crops.

10 **Lucky ankh. Roll the dice again.** Amulets are worn to keep you safe. Ankh means "life", and ankhs are the most common type of amulet.

9 **You've been playing leapfrog with your friends. Leap forwards 2 places.** From time to time, you'll get to play with other children. Enjoy it while you can!

8

Hobby horse

7 **Ride forwards 1 place on your hobby horse.** This toy came to Egypt with the Romans when they made it part of their empire.

19

20 **You've been stung by a scorpion! Go back 3 places.** Scorpions are very dangerous, so beware! They don't just live in the desert, they hide in houses, too.

Scorpion

21

22 **There's been a bumper harvest! Go forwards 4 places.** Extra grain is stored away just in case next year's harvest isn't so good.

26

25 **Your family is rich, so you get to go to school! Go forwards 3 places.** You've got it made! Learning to read and write will let you climb the ladder of success.

24 **You fell into the River Nile and were chased by a hungry crocodile! Go back 10 places.**

23

Crocodile

29 **You beat your friend at senet. Move forwards 1 place.** Being good at this board game means you're very smart and logical – you'll go far!

29 **Big day! You've had your head shaved. Jump to the finish.** You're leaving childhood behind. Now you can be just like your parents and wear a wig!

You've now made it through childhood.

Well done! It's not easy to make it this far. Try your hardest, take every opportunity, and if the king hears your name you will be blessed.

FINISH

Hieroglyphs

In Ancient Egypt, words were written with picture signs called hieroglyphs. Each sign looked like an animal, person, or thing. There were more than 700 different hieroglyphs and most, like the 25 signs shown here, stand for sounds.

(a as in hat)
Egyptian vulture

(i as in hill)
Reed leaf

(y as in happy)
Double reed leaf

(oo as in too or w as in wind)
Quail chick

(b as in bed)
Leg

(p as in pen)
Box

(m as in man)
Owl

(n as in nail)
Water

(r as in rope)
Mouth

This is the hieroglyph.

This is roughly the sound the hieroglyph makes.

This is what the hieroglyph represents.

(h as in house)
House

(h as in heel)
Twisted flax

(h as in loch)
We don't know!

(s as in sun)
Door bolt

(sh as in sheep)
Pool

(c as in cat)
Basket

(g as in garden)
Jar stand

(tch as in itch)
Tethering rope

(d as in dog)
Hand

Writing

Not many people could read and write in Ancient Egypt – it was a special skill. The Egyptians wrote with signs, called hieroglyphs, which they thought the gods had invented. It took experts a long time to figure out how to read hieroglyphs because they can stand for sounds or the picture they show.

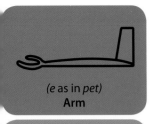

(e as in pet)
Arm

(f as in finger or v as in vet)
Horned viper

(l as in light)
Lion

(kh as in ankh)
Animal belly

(k as in kick or q as in queen)
Hill slope

(t as in time)
Loaf of bread

(j as in jam)
Cobra

Egyptian phrasebook

Egyptian words were made up of sound and meaning signs. There were sounds like our vowels, but these weren't always written down, so pronouncing words is guesswork! Silent meaning signs help us to understand the words they're beside. Can you spot any familiar signs in the phrases below?

"Don't worry!"
"em senej"

This sign stands for three sounds: *s*, *n*, and *j*.

A silent meaning sign tells us that the word it's beside is to do with speaking.

"Be quiet!"
"ger"

"Be careful!"
"ir heroo"

This sign stands for two sounds: *i* and *r*.

This silent meaning sign of a scroll tells us that something must be explained in words as there is no picture of it.

Rosetta Stone

The Rosetta Stone, found near Rosetta, in Egypt, is special because it has the same message written on it in three different languages: hieroglyphic, demotic (another Egyptian language), and Ancient Greek. Before it was discovered, no one knew what hieroglyphs meant. Jean-François Champollion, a French scholar, worked out the Egyptian by comparing it to the Greek. He had unlocked the secret of hieroglyphs!

Interview with...

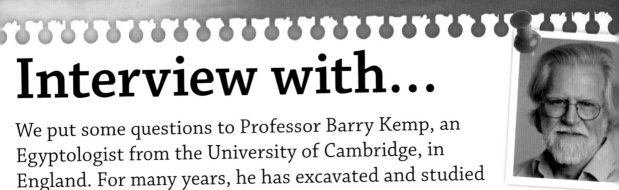

We put some questions to Professor Barry Kemp, an Egyptologist from the University of Cambridge, in England. For many years, he has excavated and studied the ancient city of Amarna, which was briefly the capital of Ancient Egypt during the reign of King Akhenaten.

Q: We know it is something to do with Egypt, but what do you actually do?

A: I have led a research team at the city of Tell el-Amarna [usually shortened to Amarna] in Egypt since 1977. We make maps, excavate houses and graves, and sometimes repair buildings.

Q: Why did you become an Egyptologist?

A: My father was a soldier in Egypt during World War II. He visited some of the ancient sites and sent back pictures. They became part of my growing up. At school, I used them in a history project, and this sparked a lifelong love of Ancient Egypt.

Q: What is special about Amarna?

A: It was founded around 1350BCE by King Akhenaten, who was married to Queen Nefertiti, but abandoned not long after his death. Its brief existence offers a unique snapshot of life in an ancient capital city.

Q: What equipment do you use?

A: We use the kind of equipment you would see on excavations in many countries: small trowels, sieves, wheelbarrows, tape measures, and so on.

Q: What are the best and worst parts of your job?

A: The best parts are being at the site and also working on the records afterwards. The worst aspect is having to do this on limited funds.

Q: Is Akhenaten your favourite pharaoh?

A: I study Akhenaten because he founded the city and his influence is everywhere, but I am more interested in the lives of his subjects.

Q: What is the most exciting thing you have ever discovered?

A: I find excitement in uncovering evidence and trying to make sense of it. At Amarna, we have the houses of the people and, from their cemeteries, evidence for their often poor state of health and brief lives.

Sun worshippers
Akhenaten built Amarna for his sun god, the Aten. The king is shown here with Nefertiti standing behind him, worshipping the god.

Archaeologists work on the site where Amarna's main temple once stood.

Tomb of a scribe
The tomb cut into this cliff close to Amarna belonged to the scribe Ahmose, who worked for Akhenaten.

WOW!

Akhenaten was the **father** of the famous boy-king **Tutankhamun.**

Studying Egypt

For more than 2,000 years, people have been visiting Egypt to learn about its history. Often in the past, ancient buildings were badly damaged by souvenir hunters only interested in finding treasure. The methods used today to study Egypt cause much less damage.

Excavation

Digging in the ground for ancient tombs and buildings, and other signs of human activity is called excavation. It must be done slowly and carefully to avoid damaging any finds.

Early Egyptologists

Giovanni Belzoni, 1778–1823
Italian explorer Belzoni made many great discoveries, including the tomb of the pharaoh Seti I.

Flinders Petrie, 1853–1942
Englishman Petrie realised the importance of carefully preserving the ancient objects he found in Egypt.

Howard Carter, 1874–1939
Carter, also English, became world famous for discovering Tutankhamun's tomb and treasures.

Curse of the tomb!

Egyptian tombs had curses written on their walls, warning people not to disturb them. Lord Carnarvon, pictured right with Howard Carter, was present at the opening of Tutankhamun's tomb, in 1922, and died a few months later. Coincidence or curse?

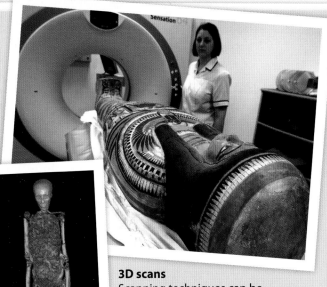

Scientific techniques

Nowadays, we can see inside mummies without unwrapping them. We can look beneath the ground with radar and see where buildings once stood by studying satellite images.

3D scans

Scanning techniques can be used to look inside wrapped mummies, through each layer of wrapping down to the body.

X-rays

X-rays of mummies can show us the skeleton under the wrappings. A few X-rays have revealed fake mummies – with sticks and stones inside rather than bones.

Satellite images

Images taken by satellites high in the sky let us see the outlines of buried buildings, which are hard to see on the ground.

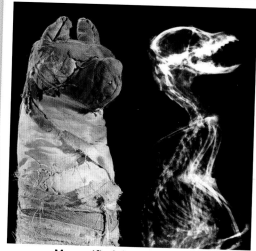

Mummified dog and its X-ray

Satellite image of the pyramids at Giza

REALLY?

Early explorers used **dynamite** to get inside the pyramids!

Egyptian facts and figures

The Egyptians achieved a lot over 3,000 years. Here are some amazing facts you might not know about them!

Missing parts

If a person had missing body parts, such as fingers or toes, they would be replaced with wooden ones for burial.

Scarab beetle

THIRSTY WORK

The world's oldest brewery was in Hierakonpolis, Egypt – it could produce 455 litres (100 gallons) of beer a day!

Mummified dung

In the Late Period, over 30 different animals were mummified, and even dung balls made by scarab beetles.

4 days is the time it took to unwrap one mummy of a noblewoman. She was covered in 14 sheets, 80 bandages, 12 cloth pads, and four sets of linen binding cords.

3,000 years is how long Egypt was ruled by pharaohs.

Tutankhamun

AKHENATEN IS THE ONLY PHARAOH TO BE SHOWN EATING AND DRINKING IN ART!

Creature chaos

What was the animal sacred to the god Seth? Over 20 different suggestions have been made, from aardvark to zebra. However, look at his arrow-shaped tail – he's definitely not real!

ABOUT
2,300,000
STONE BLOCKS MAKE UP THE GREAT PYRAMID.

It took 10 years for explorer **Howard Carter** to empty **Tutankhamun's tomb.**

Pile of objects found in Tutankhamun's tomb

SECRET MESSAGES

No one can crack the hieroglyphic code used by priests in the temple of Esna – one of their hymns is written almost entirely with crocodile signs!

587
servants were buried with King Djer.

10
was the number of days in an Ancient Egyptian week.

Glossary

Here are the meanings of some words that are useful for you to know when learning about Ancient Egypt.

amulet Magical pendant worn to protect you from harm

archaeologist Someone who looks for ancient places and objects

Ba Part of the Ancient Egyptian spirit with a human face but the body of a bird

bezel Stone or jewel positioned at the centre of a finger ring

canopic jar Jar used to store a mummy's body organs

cartouche Oval shape with a line at one end drawn or carved around the name of a king

casing blocks Smooth stone blocks of fine quality used on the outside walls of pyramids

cataracts Six natural, rocky barriers interrupting the River Nile's flow in Nubia, starting at Aswan

chariot Two-wheeled vehicle pulled by horses, used by the Egyptians in battles to shoot arrows or throw spears from

delta Fan-shaped area of fertile green land in the north of Egypt, on the Mediterranean coast

Model boat with sail and rudder

dynasty Family of kings, used as a way to sort the order of Ancient Egyptian history

Egyptologist Someone who studies Ancient Egypt

empire Large area with different peoples, ruled by a king or emperor

faience Special type of clay made in different colours, moulded into shapes and baked hard

false door Part of a wall carved into a door shape to let friendly spirits into a building

flax Green plant with long stalks that can be made into linen or rope

Greco-Roman Period Final period of Ancient Egyptian history, first with the Greek Ptolemies in power and then the Roman emperors

hieroglyph Picture sign used in Egyptian writing

incense Sticky paste burned to create perfumed smoke in temples to please the gods

Intermediate Period Unsettled period of time without a king in charge of the whole of Egypt

Inundation Annual flooding that caused the River Nile to burst its banks

Late Period Period of Egyptian history when the last Egyptian kings ruled Egypt (715–332BCE)

lotus Type of waterlily sacred to the Egyptians

Middle Kingdom Period of Egyptian history when many powerful kings ruled (1975–1755BCE)

mummification Process of making a mummy, drying and wrapping a body to preserve it

New Kingdom Period of Ancient Egypt's history when its empire grew much bigger (1540–1075BCE)

Nile River that runs through the length of Egypt and down into what was Nubia

nomad Person who moves from place to place rather than staying in a town

Nubia Egypt's neighbour to the south, often an enemy but sometimes a trading partner

obelisk Tall, needle-shaped block of stone with a shining golden tip, usually carved with hieroglyphs

Wooden shabti

Old Kingdom Period of Egyptian history when the pyramids were built (2650–2175BCE)

papyrus Name of the green marsh plant and the paper made from its stalks

pharaoh Egyptian name for the king, meaning "great house"

pylon Entrance into a temple with large towers on each side

pyramid Four-sided building with a pointed top, used in Ancient Egypt for burying dead kings

rudder Large oars at the back of a boat that are used to steer it

sarcophagus Stone coffin usually holding one or more smaller coffins inside it

scribe Someone whose job involved reading and writing

shabti Small servant statue that magically came to life and worked for their owner in the afterlife

shrine Shelter for a god's statue, which was sometimes made of gold

silt Fertile soil carried by the River Nile and left behind on its banks after a flood

sphinx Creature with a person's head (usually the king) and an animal's body (usually a lion)

stele Stone tablet, often round-topped, carved or painted with words and images

temple Home for a god or gods and a place for worshipping them

uraeus Cobra figure poised for attack, worn on the crowns of kings and gods

Index

Acknowledgements

The publisher would like to thank the following for their assistance in the preparation of this book:
Abi Wright and Molly Lattin for design assistance, Jagtar Singh and Mohammad Rizwan for cutouts, Polly Goodman for proofreading, Helen Peters for compiling the index, Bolton Library and Museum Services for the provision of artefacts for photography, Carolyn Routledge for assistance in arranging for artefacts to be photographed, Norman Taylor for photography, and Daniel Long, Dan Crisp, and Ed Merrit for illustrations. The publisher would also like to thank Professor Barry Kemp of the Amarna Trust (www.amarnatrust.com) for the "Interview with…" interview.

The publisher would like to thank the following for their kind permission to reproduce their photographs:

(Key: a-above; b-below/bottom; c-centre; f-far; l-left; r-right; t-top)

2 Dorling Kindersley: Bolton Library and Museum Services (bc, cb). **Getty Images:** Alessandro Vannini / Corbis Historical (crb). **3 Alamy Stock Photo:** Ian M. Butterfield (Egypt) (bl); Ivy Close Images (bc). **Dorling Kindersley:** Bolton Library and Museum Services (c); Alex Wilson / Rough Guides (tr); Cairo Museum (br). **4 Alamy Stock Photo:** Sputnik (bc). **Dorling Kindersley:** The Science Museum, London (cr). **5 Alamy Stock Photo:** ASP Geolmaging / NASA (tl); Peter Horree (cl). **Dorling Kindersley:** Bolton Library and Museum Services (r). **Getty Images:** De Agostini Picture Library (bc). **6 Dorling Kindersley:** Dan Crisp (ftr, cra, fcra, c, cr, cb, bc, br). **7 Dorling Kindersley:** Dan Crisp (fcla, clb, bl). **Getty Images:** Religious Images / UIG / Universal Images Group (cra). **8 Dorling Kindersley:** Dan Crisp (tl, ca, cr, crb, fcrb). **9 Dorling Kindersley:** Dan Crisp (fcl, cla, cl, c, cr, bl, br). **10 Getty Images:** DEA / A. Jemolo / De Agostini (cra). **10-11 Alamy Stock Photo:** Gianni Dagli Orti / The Art Archive. **11 Alamy Stock Photo:** World History Archive (fbr). **The Trustees of the British Museum:** (fcr, br). **Dreamstime.com:** Woverwolf (cr). **Getty Images:** DEA / S. Vannini / De Agostini Picture Library (tc). **12 Alamy Stock Photo:** Ian M. Butterfield (Egypt) (cr). **Getty Images:** DEA / G. Dagli Orti / De Agostini (c). **13 Alamy Stock Photo:** Gianni Dagli Orti / The Art Archive (tl); Pictures Colour Library / Travel Pictures (br). **Dorling Kindersley:** Cairo Museum (clb). **14 Getty Images:** DEA / S. Vannini / De Agostini Picture Library (l). **The Art Archive:** British Museum, London / Werner Forman Archive (bc). **15 Alamy Stock Photo:** Quint & Lox / Artokoloro Quint Lox Limited (tr). **16-17 Dorling Kindersley:** Daniel Long. **17 Getty Images:** PHAS / Universal Images Group (tr). **18 Dorling Kindersley:** Dan Crisp (cl, cr, bl, br). **19 Dorling Kindersley:** Dan Crisp (t, cl, cr, br). **20 Mary Evans Picture Library:** (tl, cl). **21 Mary Evans Picture Library:** (cla, ca, tr, cr, bl). **22 Alamy Stock Photo:** Reinhard Dirscherl (tr); World History Archive (bl). **Getty Images:** DEA / G. Sioen / De Agostini (cr). **23 Getty Images:** De Agostini / A. Jemolo / De Agostini Picture Library (tc); Werner Forman / Universal Images Group (c); DEA / S. Vannini / De Agostini Picture Library (br). **24-25 Dorling Kindersley:** Daniel Long. **25 Alamy Stock Photo:** Magica (bc). **26 Alamy Stock Photo:** Gianni Dagli Orti / The Art Archive (cr). **Getty Images:** De Agostini / A. Dagli Orti / De Agostini Picture Library (cr). **27 Dorling Kindersley:** Bolton Library and Museum Services (fclb); Durham University Oriental Museum (clb); University of Pennsylvania Museum of Archaeology and Anthropology (r). **29 Getty Images:** DEA / A. Dagli Orti / De Agostini Picture Library (tr). **30-31 Alamy Stock Photo:** Jan Wlodarczyk. **30 Dorling Kindersley:** Eddie Gerald / Rough Guides (bc). **Getty Images:** Glowimages (clb). **31 Alamy Stock Photo:** Nigel Westwood (br). **Dorling**

Kindersley: Eddie Gerald / Rough Guides (bl). **32 Alamy Stock Photo:** Travelpass Photography (r). **Getty Images:** Alessandro Vannini / Corbis Historical (bc). **33 Alamy Stock Photo:** Travelpass Photography (l); Ariadne Van Zandbergen (r). **34 Alamy Stock Photo:** Gianni Dagli Orti / The Art Archive (c). **Dorling Kindersley:** Bolton Library and Museum Services (br). **35 The Trustees of the British Museum:** (t). **Dorling Kindersley:** Bolton Library and Museum Services (ca, cra, fcra, cr, br); The Science Museum, London (bl). **36 Alamy Stock Photo:** Prisma Archivo (bl). **Dorling Kindersley:** Ashmolean Museum, Oxford (c); University of Aberdeen (cl); Bolton Library and Museum Services (br). **36-37 Dorling Kindersley:** Bolton Library and Museum Services (c). **37 Alamy Stock Photo:** Robert Harding Productions (t). **Dorling Kindersley:** Bolton Library and Museum Services (c, fbl, fclb, bl, crb, fcrb); Canterbury City Council, Museums and Galleries (bc). **Getty Images:** DEA Picture Library / De Agostini (br). **38 Alamy Stock Photo:** H. Peter (cr); World History Archive (c). **The Trustees of the British Museum:** (fcra, fcr). **Dorling Kindersley:** University of Pennsylvania Museum of Archaeology and Anthropology (cra, br). **39 Alamy Stock Photo:** Ivy Close Images (tc); The Print Collector (bc). **40 Dorling Kindersley:** Dan Crisp (b). **40-41 Dorling Kindersley:** Dan Crisp (b). **41 Alamy Stock Photo:** Monty Rakusen / Cultura Creative (RF) (br). **Dorling Kindersley:** Dan Crisp (cla). **Getty Images:** Felbert+Eickenberg / Stock4B (tr). **42 Alamy Stock Photo:** Blickwinkel / Koenig (c). **Dorling Kindersley:** Bolton Library and Museum Services (fcra). **43 Dorling Kindersley:** Sarah Ashun (cl); Jerry Young (tc); Durham University Oriental Museum (cb); Canterbury City Council, Museums and Galleries (fbl). **44 123RF.com:** Eric Isseleee / isseleee (c); Shlomo Polonsky / slavapolo (cl). **Dorling Kindersley:** Alex Wilson / Rough Guides (bl). **45 Dorling Kindersley:** Bolton Library and Museum Services (ca, fcra, cr, crb). **Getty Images:** Panoramic Images (cl). **46-47 Dorling Kindersley:** Daniel Long. **48 123RF.com:** Anatolii Tsekhmister / tsekhmister (cr). **Dorling Kindersley:** Bolton Library and Museum Services (bl). **49 The Trustees of the British Museum:** (tc, cra, cr). **50 Alamy Stock Photo:** Art Media / The Print Collector (tr); Pietro Scozzari / age fotostock (br). **Dorling Kindersley:** C M Dixon / AAA Collection / Ancient Art & Architecture Collection Ltd (cb); Durham University Oriental Museum (c). **50-51 The Trustees of the British Museum:** (c). **51 Alamy Stock Photo:** Gianni Dagli Orti / The Art Archive (tr). **Dorling Kindersley:** Bolton Library and Museum Services (tl, cr). **53 123RF.com:** Pitchayarat Chootai / pitchayarat2514 (tr); F. Javier Espuny / fxegs (br). **54 Andreas Mesli:** (tr). **Getty Images:** DEA / S. Vannini / De Agostini Picture Library (bc). **54-55 Getty Images:** De Agostini / G. Sioen / De Agostini Picture Library. **55 Barry Kemp:** (tl). **56 Alamy Stock Photo:** David Cole (fbl); Mary Evans Picture Library (fcl); Granger, NYC. / Granger Historical Picture Archve (fclb). **Getty Images:** GraphicaArtis / Hulton Archive (cr). **57 Getty Images:** DigitalGlobe (bl). **Press Association Images:** AP / HO / Supreme Council of Antiquities / AP (cla); John Stillwell / PA Archive (tl). **Science Photo Library:** Thierry Berrod, Mona Lisa Production (cr). **58 Dorling Kindersley:**

Bolton Library and Museum Services (ca); Alex Wilson / Rough Guides (cl); Cairo Museum (br). **Getty Images:** Marwan Naamani / AFP (tr). **59 Alamy Stock Photo:** David Cole (c); Mike P. Shepherd (bc). **Dorling Kindersley:** Dan Crisp (br). **60 Alamy Stock Photo:** The Print Collector (tl). **Dorling Kindersley:** The Science Museum, London (bl). **61 Dorling Kindersley:** University of Pennsylvania Museum of Archaeology and Anthropology (tc). **62 Alamy Stock Photo:** Gianni Dagli Orti / The Art Archive (tl).

Cover images: *Front:* **Alamy Stock Photo:** Quint & Lox / Artokoloro Quint Lox Limited cra/ (Snake Bracelet); **Bridgeman Images:** Cleveland Museum of Art, OH, USA / Gift of the John Huntington Art and Polytechnic Trust bl; **Dorling Kindersley:** Bolton Library and Museum Services crb, crb/ (beads), Newcastle Great Northern Museum, Hancock cra; **Getty Images:** DEA Picture Library / De Agostini cr; *Back:* **Dorling Kindersley:** Bolton Library and Museum Services cr, Bolton Library and Museum Services tr, Canterbury City Council, Museums and Galleries cla, The Science Museum, London clb; *Front Flap:* **Alamy Stock Photo:** World History Archive cr; **Dorling Kindersley:** Bolton Library and Museum Services clb, cl, clb/ (inside), Bolton Library and Museum Services c, Bolton Library and Museum Services c/ (glass bottle), Bolton Library and Museum Services t, Bolton Library and Museum Services crb/ (inside), Cairo Museum bl, University of Aberdeen br, University of Pennsylvania Museum of Archaeology and Anthropology cla; **Getty Images:** DEA / S. Vannini / De Agostini Picture Library ca; *Back Flap:* **Dorling Kindersley:** Natural History Museum, London clb, University of Aberdeen tl; *Front Endpapers:* **Alamy Stock Photo:** Collection Dagli Orti / The Art Archive (1950BCE); Gianni Dagli Orti / The Art Archive (1840BCE); Ivy Close Images (1540BCE); Joana Kruse (2550BCE); Magica (1500BCE); Prisma Archivo (1540BCE); World History Archive (4000BCE). **Dorling Kindersley:** Dan Crisp (1630BCE); Eddie Gerald / Rough Guides (1910BCE). *Back Endpapers:* **Alamy Stock Photo:** Ian M. Butterfield (Egypt) (1350BCE); Gianni Dagli Orti / The Art Archive (332BCE); Nedko Dimitrov (130CE); Angus McComiskey (1457BCE); Prisma Archivo (1155BCE); Realy Easy Star / Toni Spagone (1480BCE); Lizzie Shepherd / robertharding (END); Stapleton Historical Collection / Heritage Image Partnership Ltd (1274BCE). **Dorling Kindersley:** Cairo Museum (1332BCE).

All other images © Dorling Kindersley
For further information see: www.dkimages.com

My Findout facts:

Timeline of Ancient Egypt

Thutmosis III
Thutmosis III comes to the throne very young, with his stepmother Hatshepsut at his side. She shares his kingship for 15 years.

Ramses in his chariot

Tutankhamun
The boy-king Tutankhamun becomes pharaoh. His reign is brief, but his legend will live on.

Stalemate!
Ramses II fights the Hittites at Kadesh. He claims victory, but is lucky to escape with his life!

Changes in rulers
Collapse of the New Kingdom. Priest-kings rule Thebes; Libyans rule the north.

| 1480BCE | 1457BCE | 1350BCE | 1332BCE | 1274BCE | 1155BCE | 1075BCE |

← Continued from front of book

Disaster!
Akhenaten turns Egypt upside down, closing temples and founding a new capital and a new religion.

Ramses III
The wives of Ramses III try to murder him.

Victory!
Thutmosis III defeats the Mitanni at the Battle of Megiddo.

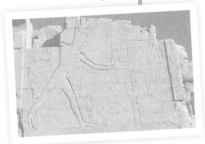

A huge figure of the king holds his enemies by the hair.